T0366031

Soulful
DEVOTIONS

DOMINIQUE

AuthorHouse™
1663 Liberty Drive
Bloomington, IN 47403
www.authorhouse.com
Phone: 1 (800) 839-8640

Published by AuthorHouse 04/11/2019

ISBN: 978-1-5462-7974-7 (sc)
ISBN: 978-1-5462-7975-4 (e)

Library of Congress Control Number: 2019901814

Print information available on the last page.

authorHOUSE®

Acknowledgments

Soulful Devotions is a poetry book inspired by the ups and downs of life. Life is full of twists and turns and obstacles we all must overcome; the book captures the lessons I have learned through my personal experiences. I hope this book will help people find relief and give hope that they, too, can overcome challenging obstacles. Readers from different backgrounds will find poems they can relate to. The goal of *Soulful Devotions* is to promote healing and joy in the lives of others. I want to thank Our Heavenly Father for the inspiration and words of my book. He is the reason this book exists. Also, I would like to dedicate this book to the women in my family who came before me. Thank you, Mom, Cynthia, Granny, and Nneka for your love and guidance. You all are such vital parts of my life!

I hope you enjoy exploring *Soulful Devotions* and find what you are looking for.

Dominique

CONTENTS OF SOUL

GOD

Faith   Strength

Hope   Resilience

PHASE 1: PAIN

Freeing My Soul

I got to free my soul, cut loose the bondage you once put on me,

Let go of this anger and genuinely wish you well and see you out of my life for good.

I want to let go of thoughts and feelings of inadequacies and stop living in the past,

Wondering if there was anything else I could have done?

I ask God to free my soul and, for once in my life, make me whole.

Help me, Lord, to channel my anger, pain, hurt, and despair into something positive, beautiful, and uplifting,

Washing away the old me as the new one comes to be.

The girl you knew is no longer; she died along with the dream you sold her.

When I decided to leave, I did not know where I was going, but knew I had to get out!

I was a shell of me, like a damn robot, merely existing and numbing myself to certain feelings.

Being numb for so long has finally taken its toll on me, and now I'm starting to feel the aftermath. God, please bring me relief; please keep my spirit all the way up.

God, free me, I'm pleading, because I know this is greater than me. I thank you for opening up my eyes to the possibilities and giving me transparency, because, for a while, I was in a trance, covered in lies, deceit, and manipulation, which had me in autopilot; I was a robot, a shell of me. I look back and thank you, God, for delivering me.

IS PAIN LOVE?

I was once told love is kind, patient, understanding, and unconditional,

But the fact is

I have never felt this feeling from the men in my life.

For me, love has been pain.

Love for me has been hard,

A constant fight, trying to prove myself worthy,

A struggle,

That resulted in bondage,

Being abused mentally, physically, and emotionally.

This type of love almost killed me.

Never quite feeling as if I were enough,

Never good enough.

Love did not build me up,

Love tried to destroy me.

I was love's new conquest, and eventually it conquered me in the worst way.

It took my mind,

Had me thinking differently.

It made me numb.

Love was the center of my world.

I needed constant gratification.

Was not sure who I was,

Glamorized the wrong things.

NUMB

My heart, heavy with numbness from all the pain caused,

No longer feeling anything.

I realized in life you should not feel everything.

Some things are better left numb, because if I still felt them, I might want to act on my feelings
and give in to the insanity,

Repay some people for all the pain they caused me.

Feeling lost, wondering whom can I trust in a world so lost and dark.

God, please do not let them corrupt my soul.

Some things are better left numb, because if I still felt them, they would have me on a watch
from all the pain caused,

Bad memories that come from time to time,

The scars that bruised my soul,

My internal proof.

All this pain bottled up inside; trying to suppress it so it does not explode.

Feeling numb might not be so bad after all.

Feeling numb is my necessity and armor against this cold world.

Mistaking my kindness as weakness,

Dogging me out because you could,

Not realizing you had a diamond in a world full of rhinestones,

Never saw my true potential.

Numb!

Sums up the extreme pain buried deep inside.

Finding myself, recovering and uncovering from the smoke I inhaled, the vapors of negativity

    I took in at the hands of you, someone I held close,

You taught me how to be.

I no longer put myself all the way out,

This means being more cautious,

Because I know the risk, and that price is too high.

One must prove worthy before they even get a feeling from me!

PAIN

Pain has been the common theme for my life,
How about you?
Pain has made me feel alive.
It's such a shame to become accustomed to the fights and daily struggle.
Seems as if I can't get right.

I have too much on my mind.
I'm unable to concentrate,
Trying to stay focus and keep my eyes on the prize.
Right now, it seems as if the more I try to stay on the straight and narrow, daggers are
    constantly being thrown my way.
I'm reminded, however, that these daggers are just a part of war:
Good vs. evil.

We all know the outcome—I'm not worried.
I'm going somewhere, and people cannot stand that.
I'm not going to lie—it gets hard to see past my current circumstances, especially when real
    life comes to play,
I constantly get tested, sometimes multiple times a day however I refuse to lose and get up to
    fight for another day.

So many responsibilities wrapped around my neck, trying to suffocate me,

Trying to suck all my dreams and hopes away.

Pain, you trying me,

But I will not let you conquer me.

THIN LINE

It's a thin line between love and hate.

It was all good just a week ago.

It was all good when I was unsure of who I was.

Now that I'm stepping into who I'm supposed to be, problems suddenly surrounds me.

My inner circle is much smaller.

When did the love escape and the hate creep in?

Was it when you took me for granted?

Or was it

When I became more comfortable in my own skin?

Why does love turn to hate?

Two opposite extremes,

Meet in the middle.

Then it all goes bad.

Poof! Just like that, the narrative changed.

Please explain,

Because the lines are blurry.

It's hard to tell.

The ones who once loved you now hate you.

How does that happen?

Does poison get in their veins and infect their brains?

Keep the poison away from me.

It is dangerous.

Lord, keep my veins pure.

Love flows in and out.

Hate has no place.

No time to waste.

Hate makes you weak.

It can't make you great.

It takes your mind,

Has you thinking differently.

When hate takes over, the results are not great.

The same ones I thought loved me,

Showed their true colors,

When I came into myself and wanted more—why is that?

It's a thin line between love and hate.

Be grateful for the few in your corner who have genuine love and support you.

PHASE 2: HEARTBREAK

CAPTIVITY

Why is my mind being held captive?

Let me go, and set me free,

I'm tired of negative thoughts and past what-ifs playing over and over again in my head like
   a broken record.

Let me go, and set me free.

Why do I have to think how you want me to?

My mind is my own,

It belongs to me!

Some days, I feel as if I'm in a mental prison,

Waiting to be set free,

I'm tired of seeing these barriers in my way.

Every day, I try to be positive, but it seems as though negativity always creeps in.

Who left the door open?

Give me some peace.

Let me go, and set me free.

Or …

Do I hold the key?

Lord, please give me the answer,

I just want to be free.

NEVER ENOUGH

You want me back now?

Why now?

When you had me, I was never good enough for you.

Always going out of my way for your love,

To the point where I do not even want it now.

Keep it!

Give it to someone else.

Your love is toxic,

Toxic to the core, you know, bad for the soul.

Your love made me doubt myself,

Had me double-checking myself,

Looking in the mirror differently, not recognizing the person looking back.

Love from you was too hard to come by, so keep it.

Since we have been apart,

I've been holding my head high, looking in the mirror and loving what I see,

So why invite back toxic energy?

For what purposes?

Because the love I have for you outweighs the love I have for myself?

Trust and believe you are not worth my love, peace of mind and confidence.

I thank God for closing the door on us so because I became a better version of myself.

PHASE 3: REALIZATION

STRENGTH

What is strength?

Is strength hurting someone, or is it being the bigger person and restraining yourself?

I guess it depends on whom you ask.

My strength is tested day after day,

I catch it from every angle to the point that I contemplate,

"Is it even worth it?"

Sometimes, I want to say, "Forget it," and throw my hands up.

But then where would I be?

I'm starting to think strength is getting back up after being knocked down,

Pushing through even when it is painful,

Keeping your head up when you are too tired to hold it up,

Seeing success as the only option.

Strength—

How much can one person take?

I've been strong my entire life;

I cannot recall a time when I was weak.

Strength comes from circumstances.

As diamonds are made from pressure,

I grew into the person I am today because of my circumstances and the pressures placed on me.

I see winning and conquering challenges as the only options.

The journey to get there is trying;

It will test you at every turn.

So put on your seatbelt, and get ready for the ride.

GLASS HOUSES

What are glass houses made of?

It seems glass houses are made of harsh judgment, hypocrisy, jealousy, hate, and negativity.

People who live in glass houses want to discuss everyone's business except their own;

They can find something wrong with everyone except the person staring back at them in the mirror.

Glass houses are built on insecurities;

Glass houses are fake, just like the people who live in them.

People who live in glass houses do the worst things and bury them in their backyards, but the first chance they get to blast others, they take it.

Instead of being a part of the solution by helping others,

They'd rather tear people down who need encouragement.

People who live in glass houses are miserable;

Their only joy is bringing others down.

Do you live in a glass house?

If so, get out!

You might feel you are on top now, but give it some time, and you will realize you got played.

Instead of living your life,

You observe others;

You will soon figure out you are the fool.

Live and let live.

Be the light.

Encourage, uplift, and help build instead of trying to destroy, because eventually what you put out will come back, like a boomerang, and shatter your house.

SACRIFICES

Sacrifices must be made.
Hurdles must be overcame,
Obstacles pushed out of the way.
Full speed ahead—
No one stopping me,
Because I know where I'm going.
Feet planted on the ground,
Head held up high,
My foundation solid,
The only way I can go from here is up!

LOVE

Love is something to cherish.
Love is hard to find.
Love takes time.
Love is something to hold on to.

Love makes the difference.
Love makes you listen.
Love makes you want to become a better person.

Love transforms you.
Love starts from within.
Cherish love and realize how far it got you,
Because without it,
Where would you be?

TAKEOFF

Get up!
Get going!
Get up!
Get going!
Your plane is here,
And
Takeoff is in five minutes.
You are not ready?
What do you mean?
Hurry up!
Get up!
Get going!
Planes do not come around here often.
Most will never have a plane,
So
Get up
And own the moment—

Or

The next time you see a plane,

It is not going to be for you!

Remember to cherish the moment.

Be grateful, because only a few get to experience something so special,

So live in the moment.

DREAMS

Turning my dreams into my reality.

Growing up, no one told me it would be this hard for my dreams to come true.

It appears you must make a choice.

One cannot have both;

You are either taking the regular route or daring to be different and live outside the box.

We all have dreams.

Some are okay leaving it at that, while others are not.

My dreams will not let me rest.

My dreams are my fire;

They are the reason I get up day after day.

I feel this fire in my belly;

It fuels me every day.

When times get tough and I want to throw my hands up, I feel intense pain in my gut.

Boom!

An explosion, saying, "Get up and go get it."

The time is now.

My dreams remind me my current circumstances are temporary and that this too shall pass.

I cannot let go of my dream, because I refuse to be another lost soul.

No, that route is not for me.

My dreams are the reason I wake up; without them, I wonder if I would survive.

CHOICES

In the city, stuck between two choices,
Do I?
Will I?
Should I?
Or
Do I walk away?
Stuck in the middle,
Not sure which way to turn,
Realizing the risk associated with each; however, I'm looking for the best option, so which
    outweighs the other?

I'm starting to realize my morals, values, and ethics are challenged by the daily choices made.
Some of the choices I know are not always "morally correct," but life forces you to do things
    you do not always want to do.
Life has a way of shaking things up.
Only the strong will survive in this dark world.
I'm learning to be flexible.

Life has forced my hands plenty of times.
I'm not the young, naive girl I used to be.

Day by day, the ideas that were once in my head about life get washed away with every decision
I make.

I'm a grown woman now, making decisions.

In the battle, I will always keep my head up, right or wrong,

Because

Life is not always so clear-cut, and I got to do what I have to—we all do!

Hopefully, on the other side, I will see the answers why and no longer secretly question every
tough decision I have been forced to make.

I'm living day by day,

Handling what life throws my way,

The best way I know how.

HIM

He's physically my type,

Eyes, lips, height,

For a minute I thought this might be right and then I stopped and realized,

He's not bringing it.

Some might call me stuck up or hard to please because I'm looking past his physical features
and he simply does not measure up.

You are older than me,

Yet, I have more to show for my life,

You can't give me anything but a good time, and I'd rather keep it between those lines,

Not trying to turn nothing into something because consequences are soon to follow,

I rather skip those problems,

You and I are on different levels not in a superficial way but something deeper than that more
in a spiritual way.

I'm trying to go somewhere,

Be somebody,

Do things I was told I would never do,

Have a family, and you can't provide any of those things for me.

I know we all have to start out somewhere, but you should have started long ago,

Now you're behind, playing catch-up.

I know how this story goes because I have been here before.

Once the love dries up, all I will have to hold on to is excuses and promises of a better tomorrow.

No, thank you,

I choose my life,

I don't let life choose for me.

I know what I want and you do not fit,

This is not a one size fits all situation,

I appreciate you trying,

But I'm done playing games and I'm on to greater things.

I'm too grown to be playing "Ride or Die" for a man who is not worth it.

I will wait for my king,

Because I refuse to sacrifice my years, body, and time for a man who does not measure up.

EVERYTHING AIN'T WHAT IT SEEMS

Behind the smiles,

Wide eyes,

Parties,

Lies the truth.

The truth is you are not happy but too caught up with life.

Trying to believe the image you have become,

Trying your hardest not to crack under all the pressure.

Behind those smiling eyes

Are dried up tears inside, wanting everything to be fine,

But at times

Realizing it is not.

The front you've put on for so long is ready to collapse,

Rushing down,

Boom! Crash! It collapsed.

There goes the perfect image you damn near killed yourself to uphold.

Instead of focusing on your real happiness,

You got caught up in the superficial.

Didn't you know that is a mere fantasy?

It disappears day by day with life.

When the illusion fades,

Real life still stays.

Stop getting so easily caught up with others' perceptions, because if you are in too deep you
drown in it.

Stop and think and be true to yourself!

RAISING MY SON

When you were a little girl, did you dream of one day having a family?

Yes, when I was little, I wanted a huge family, not knowing what it took to raise a child. The fantasy I had growing up is not my reality. My reality is far different from what I pictured before. Raising my son is the most challenging job I have ever had.

I remember when I was pregnant and wanting a son, not realizing what I was truly asking for. When my son was younger, and to this day, people always give me compliments on him, and I appreciate them; however, I'm waiting for the other shoe to drop.

Honestly speaking, I wonder, when are black boys done being cute or adorable and seen as something to fear? Before you go on to read the rest, I challenge you to think about the question. I dread the day my son will have to face an ignorant person in life who judges him by his appearance and claim "scared" because of their ignorant ideas of what a black boy, a young black man, and a man is. How will I explain this to him? Why should any parent have to explain ignorance to their child? All parents are afraid to raise children in this world, because we see the good and bad side of society; however, black and brown parents have ten times the fear of a white parent. We have to explain things to our children others would never think to explain. When my son asks, "Why, Mommy," what do I tell him? This is how the world is. Why must he be so different?

The world we live in is designed for the men and boys of color to fail. When they are younger, they are viewed as no threat, but when they approach adolescence, all the innocence is washed away with darkness. Why? I'm raising my son to be respectful, intelligent, caring, encouraging, and an overall good person. I'm instilling morals and values in him, but none of it matters, because most see will only see his physical appearance. Through it all, I'm teaching my son to love being black and to have thick skin, because in this world, you will need it. I'm teaching my son to know who he is so when another receives him to be a "threat," he will prove them wrong. We must teach our sons to rise above negative stereotypes. But still I wonder, how far will this go in a world designed against us?

PHASE 4: BREAKTHROUGH

BLACK WOMEN

Being a black woman is hard.
It comes with challenges you can never understand unless you are one.
As black women, we are constantly fighting to prove ourselves,
Fighting European standards of beauty, proving we are worthy and beautiful.

As black women, we hardly get to make excuses;
That's a foreign language to us.
All we know is how to get the job done.
We are the glue to our families and communities.
We hold things together.
We have to be strong when we want to be weak.
We make sure our children eat, whether they have a father or not.

Being a black woman is powerful,
We can make something out of nothing,
Our spirits rise through adversity.
We give our children encouragement while keeping it real.

We hold power in our bodies,
Our words.
We are beautiful.

We do not know how to lose.

We know how to survive despite the odds being stacked against us.

We rise,

We are bold,

Most of all, we are unbreakable!

FOUNDATION

My foundation is strong;
My foundation is built to last.
It is solid and not falling over.
My foundation gets better day by day.

My foundation was not always strong.
I had to take some time to rebuild it.
Earlier in life, I lost sight of myself;
My foundation was shaky, barely there.
At one point, the little foundation I did have became so shaky,
It was eventually destroyed.

God had to rebuild me.
He gave me the solid blocks to my foundation;
Now my foundation breaks for no one.
In life, God will allow you to be broken down so you can rebuild yourself.
I guess it is true: we all must earn our stripes in life.
With every stripe earned, my foundation has become stronger.

I no longer fear the unknown.
My foundation is strong and can handle whatever comes my way.

Take it from someone who knows:

When you are broken, lost, and confused,

Take time to rejoice, because God is giving you another chance to rebuild yourself so the next time, you are solid, and nothing will break you down!

PHONE

So, are you going to make me answer the phone?

Please stop ringing my line trying to make me realize.

I'm done listening.

I sleep well at night.

I'm no longer up late at night,

Wondering worried about what are you doing.

Let's be clear.

I do not want you.

Stop calling!

It's pointless.

You are not calling to speak with your son.

Rather, you intend to use him as a pawn.

You're calling to manipulate and weasel your way back in,

Trying to confuse me,

Still running that tired line, "Let's be a family."

I see your ways have not changed.

You're still trying to leech off me.

No, thank you!

We deserve much better than you,

A real man,

Who knows the value of family,

A real man,

Who I do not have to question,

A real man,

Who gives loves unconditionally,

A real man,

Who does not put his hands on women,

A real man,

Who wants to see me at my best,

A real man,

Who is not intimated by confidence,

A real man,

Who is not intimated by a woman, who knows her worth,

But rather is

More turned on by that fact,

A real man,

Who realizes when he has a real one by his side,

So all the others are left behind.

COUNTED ME OUT

Counted me out,

Down and out,

One, two,

Lights out!

You counted me out too fast

Didn't even give me a countdown.

Now, I'm about to show you what's up now.

Many have doubted,

Told me I will never make it,

"Forget about your dreams," some said.

The closest ones to me,

Counted me out,

Thought I was down for the count,

As if I would never rise again!

They assumed because I had my son at age seventeen, I was done,

If you asked them, they knew my fate without a doubt.

At one point, my own father doubted me.

For a long time, his words played over and over in my head,

Like a song played out.

Constantly fighting to prove myself because I'm not built to lose.

Having my child gave me something to fight for.

I have to fight for me,

My dreams,

My happiness.

I have to fight for my son.

I remember when I was seventeen and pregnant,

Feeling ashamed and embarrassed.

This period was hard for me.

At one point, it was hard for me to see past my current circumstances.

In that moment, my older brother reminded me to keep my head up.

Keep my head up with pride,

Keep pushing through.

From my experience, I have learned, if you push hard enough and refuse to give up,

You will knock down all the barriers in your way and make your nonbelievers into believers.

Don't forget to appreciate those who supported you through your ups and downs when all
the others counted you out.

STARS

The stars are aligned,

The night young and full of possibilities.

I'm strapping on my seatbelt because here I come,

Ready to conquer the world,

To live out my dreams,

Finally realizing dreams do come true and fairytales are not just make-believe.

Life is what you make it,

So get up and make it great!

WISE

A wise person once told me,

"Nothing comes to a sleeper but a dream."

If you want something, it is up to you to make it happen.

No one else,

No excuses,

Just accomplishments.

There is no room for failure,

When success is the only option.

GROWING PAINS

Growing in ways I can't believe,

Finally realizing my dreams are becoming my reality.

Growth—what a process!

At one point, I thought growth was going to get me.

It angered me,

Confused me;

It took everything that was once familiar and made it foreign.

I did not understand it.

There were times when I wanted to go back to the old days,

When things were simpler

And I was comfortable.

But then I looked at how far I had come.

Growth made me.

Growth broke me.

Some of the people closest to me tried to destroy me.

I guess they didn't get the memo;

Growth beat them to it!

Growth broke me down and rebuilt me.

Growth opened my eyes.

Slowly, I started moving away from everything that was a threat to my growth process,

Saying no to fake friends and to bum men,

Realizing my potential is unlimited and not limiting myself.

Growth is sick.

It made me sick;

It made me tired.

It made me want to throw my hands up.

SINGLE

Why are you single?
Because I refuse to settle.
You say my standards are too high and I need to lower them.
Well, I say your standards are too low and you should raise them.
I was you,
The girl too afraid of being single, plagued by thoughts of needing someone to define me!
But guess what?
It did not and does not.

Feeling incomplete and putting too much effort and energy into the wrong things led me into
   two abusive relationships, one right after the other.
Both relationships had me feeling low as dirt;
Whatever self-esteem I thought I had disappeared with every argument,
Disappeared with every blow,
Vanished!

The feeling of hopelessness overcame me.
Being so desperate for love had me down and out, not knowing which way was up.
All the tears I cried, and my swollen eyes blinded to my own worth.

At one point, I did not recognize the person looking back at me.
I could not stand the sight of her.
I knew she was the blame for all my problems;
It was all her fault until it wasn't.

Feeling pain until I could not feel it anymore—
This was my new normal.
I was okay with going through the motions,
No longer feeling anything,
Lost deep in depression;
The fog was so thick, I could not see my way out.
I guess my mama was right, but I was not going to tell her that.

Going forward, I refuse to settle, because I know what it can do.
I lived the effects of it, and it took everything to break free.
I will never travel down that road again, because that is my lesson learned.

We all must know our worth.
Believe you are worthy!
Love yourself and know a relationship does not define you;
That's simply between you and God!

HAPPY

Feeling so good.
This feeling cannot be real.
What's wrong?
For once, I feel inner peace,
Seeing the beauty in things,
Not overthinking things,
Just going along.

For once,
I am free,
Seeing my progress,
Letting go of past thoughts,
No longer feeling trapped.
The key has set me free,
I no longer feel constraints.
Finally, I can breathe now!

For once,
I feel comfortable in my own skin,
Genuinely wishing well on others,
For once, I'm happy with myself,

I can tell you this feeling, starts from within.

I thank God for making me feel complete,

God took a girl who did not love herself and made her a woman that loves herself fully!

She accepts her flaws, her stretch marks, and all because it tells the story of where she has been
and why she's so blessed!

No Apologies

I will not apologize for being myself.
I will not dim my light so yours can shine a little brighter.
I can't help the way God made me.
Take it how you want to!

No apologies given.
Screw your superficial perception of me.
It's sad you cannot look past the physical to discover there is more inside.
I'm a good person and will go out of my way to help others, but clearly all you see is me in
    my physical state, forgetting the mental and spiritual.

I will continue to embrace myself,
And the person I'm meant to be, whether you like it or not.
I'm no longer worried about what you think, because from the looks of it, you do not even
    have it together.
Stop focusing on me and get your life in order,
Learn to embrace and love yourself, and stop trying to measure up to me, because we all know
    there is only one me.
No apologies given.

BOLD WOMAN

She is fearless,

Driven,

Strong,

Sometimes scared, but you would never know it, because she hides it so well.

She does not take no for an answer.

She is persistent.

She walked through the fire and still came out ahead.

Does she have scars?

Yes, but she wears them with honor.

She takes pride in the scars she has because she values the lesson each of them has taught her.

The fire thought it was going to destroy her, take her hopes and dreams and burn them down to ashes.

The fire underestimated her power and overestimated theirs.

Did not realize she is a warrior.

She goes for whatever she wants.

Nothing will stop her or her destiny.

She has the power.

Since God is within her, she will not fall.

She remains realistic and acknowledges there are tough times ahead and her current circumstances are not the best, but she pushes ahead,

Day after day,

Moment after moment.

She is bold and lives her life unapologetically.

Bold describes her perfectly, because she lives her truth out loud, regardless if you agree.

Fearless, she is.

LETTER TO THE READERS

Thank you for reading *Soul Devotions*. I hope you enjoyed the book and it has brought some peace, inspiration, and joy into your life. Baring the soul is scary, because it leaves you vulnerable, thinking, *How will others receive me? Will they connect with me or judge me?* One does not know until they put themselves out there. It takes courage to bare your soul to another. You need some sense of self.

Nevertheless, it is still scary because of the unknown. Baring your soul is hard, because it brings back memories and feelings we try to erase and push down deep inside. Scars magically reappear, and past tragedies come rushing back to mind on cue. However, if you can empower someone with your story, isn't it worth it? I'm starting to realize that by being open, you can help others in their search for answers. Baring your soul will help treat your scars and heal others.

Vulnerability is not easy; however, being vulnerable is quite a concept, because at the end of the day, we are all humans trying to figure it out, so be open and authentic, because you do not know who you are helping or making an impact on. Never get too caught up in the superficial, because then all you will be is an empty shell.

Printed in the United States
By Bookmasters